ELIZABETH'S GLASS

206. Bale, "Epistle Dedicatory," fol.8v.

207. See Muriel C. Bradbrook, "Virtue Is the True Nobility." In *All's Well That End's Well* Helena, who is of relatively low birth but of virtuous character, and Bertram, who is of relatively high birth but of vicious character, are compared in such a way that we might wonder whether he is so far above her station as to make his marriage to her as unbearably painful to him as incestuous marriage would be. Helena is Bertram's sister-by-adoption, whom Bertram's mother the Countess would call "daughter" by transforming her into a daughter-in-law (1.3.141–56). It requires the King of France to emphasize that nobility resides in the soul, not in blood.

208. Publius Tacitus, *The Annals of Imperial Rome*, 12.42 (emphasis added). It is worth noting that Agrippina's fourfold kinship arrangement imitates to some extent that of Roman women in general, who were regarded legally "as daughters of their husbands and sisters of their children" (Giovanni Battista Vico, *Principles of New Science*, para.507). The arrangement was also like that of the old Roman "temple of Ceres, Liber, and Libera, the mother or the spouse, the son, and the daughter, of the Buddhick or Bacchic god" (Titus Livy, *The Romane History*, III.55; see Alexander Del Mar, *Ancient Britain in the Light of Modern Archaeological Discoveries*, p.101).

209. Saint Paul, among others, developed the Roman practice of adrogation of sons by their fathers into a powerful ideology of adoption by Christ, an adoption whose end was not so much "liberation" in the Roman juridical sense of the word as a homogenizing or leveling of all human beings under God the universal Father. The disappearance of the Vestal Virgins in the fourth century A.D. (under Constantine), which was a critical moment in the history of Rome, corresponded to the Roman institutionalization of Christianity as the official state religion in the same century. That is why Christian nuns have many of the rituals, powers, and obligations of the Vestal Virgins. In the Roman ceremony by which a novice became a Vestal, for example, the novice's hair was shorn; the *pontifex* or head priest called her *Amata* (Loved One); and she promised to be chaste (Aulus Gellius, *Les Nuits attiques*, 1.12).

210. Philip Butler, Introduction to Jean Racine, *Britannicus*, p.169.

211. Geoffrey of Monmouth, *Historia Regum Britanniae*, 3:1.

212. *Domina* had been an important legal term in Roman times. It meant not only *regina*, or *rex* (on the title *domina*, see esp. Richard Onslow, *Empress Maud*), but also something like "female head of the household" (*Oxford Latin Dictionary*). Eventually *domina* came to mean "the [Mother] superior of a nunnery," though it always retained some connotation of property owner-

ship, as in John Kersey's 1708 definition (*Dictionarium Anglo-Brittanicum*): "a Title formerly given to those honorable Women that held a Barony in their own right of inheritance."

213. "All this [throughout Geoffrey's work, about women ruling] is substantially unparalleled in early history, British or otherwise," writes J. S. P. Tatlock in *The Legendary History of Britain*, p.287. "In Welsh history there is no hint of it, and in France, as no reader of [Shakespeare's] *Henry V* need be told, the Salic law forbade any woman to reign."

214. Originating with the Salian Franks, the Salic law was supposedly invoked in 1316 and 1322 to exclude the daughters of the Capetian Louis X (king of Navarre, 1305–16, and king of France, 1314–16) and of the Capetian Philip V (king of France, 1316–22) from the succession to the throne. Philip VI, 1328–50, who assumed the throne after the death of the Capetian Charles IV (king of France, 1322–28), was the first of the House of the Valois, which ruled France until 1589, when Henry III died and the House of Bourbon assumed power. Marguerite of Navarre was also known as Marguerite of Valois.

215. Cf. Lisa Jardine, *Still Harping on Daughters*, chap.3, "Wealth, Inheritance, and the Spectre of Strong Women."

216. Catherine de Medici (1519–89) in 1533 married Henry, second son of Francis I of France, whose sister was Marguerite of Navarre. Catherine became queen of France in 1547; three of her four sons became kings of France. In the tradition of queen mothers ("jointresses," almost as in *Hamlet*), she ruled as regent with great power during the minority of Charles IX (1560–63) and his later reign (1563–74) and was also influential over Henry III (1574–89).

217. Bale's catalogues have been ignored even by Bale scholars: Leslie P. Fairfield, *John Bale*, does not even mention Bale's edition of Elizabeth's "Glass"; cf. H. C. McCusker, *John Bale*. Protestant reformers other than Bale, appeasing in later years the Protestant Queen Elizabeth, "dwelt more on Elizabeth's exceptional qualities than on the general worth of women"; see Travitsky, *Paradise*, p.92 (citing Doris May Stenton, *The English Women in History*, pp.126–27); Carole Levin, "Queens and Claimants"; Constance Jordan, "Feminism and the Humanists"; and John Knox's distrust of all women in his 1558 *First Blast of the Trumpet*. Lewalski, "Of God and Good Women," p.213, draws attention to Aemilia Lanyer's contribution to the so-called *querelle des femmes*. On such catalogues of good women as may have influenced Lanyer—Boccaccio's *De claris mulieribus*, Chaucer's *Legend of Good*

Women, Christine de Pizan's *Book of the City of Ladies* (cf. P. G. C. Campbell, "Christine de Pisan en Angleterre") — see also R. Kelso, *Doctrine of the Lady of the Renaissance*.

218. See Bale's remarks in Askew, *The First Examinacyon*, fol.11r; and Elaine V. Beilen, "Anne Askew's Self-Portrait in the *Examinations*," in Hannay, *Silent but for the Word*, p.85.

219. In a letter of December 6, 1559, to five Catholic bishops deprived of their sees for refusing to accept the new Church of England, Elizabeth refers to a tradition of British Christianity separate and independent from the Romish tradition. She mentions "the ancient monument of Gildas" (probably that sixth century Romano-British historian's *De excidio et conquestu Britanniae*) and such quasi-historical events as the visit to Britain of Joseph of Arimathea. Long before Augustine's arrival, she advises the Catholic bishops, there was Christianity in Britain.

220. For remarks on these and other women listed by Bale, see Glossary of Proper Names in Bale (below).

221. *Hamlet*, 1.2.9. In the Hamlet legend Gertrude is, like the Virgin Mary and like Agrippina, related fourfold to the Ruler. See my *Children of the Earth*, chap.5.

222. Tatlock, *Legendary History*, p.286.

223. "He (she) understood the custom to be rather more fitting for men than for women": Saxo Grammaticus, *Historiae Danicae*, bk.IX; cited in Tatlock, *Legendary History*, p.288.

224. Blandina's remarkable martyrdom, which took place under the Roman Emperor Marcus Aurelius in 177 A.D., is discussed by Bale in his prefaces to Askew's *Examinacyons*, fols.7v–9r. Askew was the religious and nationalist model for Bale, who in his autobiographical *Vocacyon of John Bale* "casts himself as a Protestant saint" (Fairfield, *John Bale*, p.141); see also Beilin, "Anne Askew's Self-Portrait," pp.80, 271 n.5. King (*Tudor Royal Iconography*, p.207) points out that "Blandina, Bale's specific model for Anne Askew, is presented in *Ecclesiastica historia* as a type of the Spouse of Christ."

225. Bale's "catalogues or nomenclatures of famous and honorable women" list some (including Gwendolyn and Marcia: "Conclusion," fols.42v, 43v) who became "king," a term which may be applied to a female "who rules or bears herself like a king" (OED, s.v. "King," I.3).

226. Bale, "Conclusion," fol.40v.

227. Elizabeth publicly identified with Saint Elizabeth and other Marian figures, including the Elizabeth who was the niece of Saint Anne (of the

Immaculate Conception) and the cousin of Saint Mary (of the Virgin Birth). See Roy C. Strong, *The Cult of Elizabeth*, p.125; and Robin H. Wells, *Spenser's "Faerie Queene" and the Cult of Elizabeth*, p.18. Some critics have noted that Elizabeth I was seen as the bride of Canticles and even as a *sponsa Christi*— Edmund Spenser linked "England's Eliza to the Spouse of Christ" (King, *Tudor Royal Iconography*, pp.195, 207, 261; cf. David Norbrook, *Poetry and Politics in the English Renaissance*, p.84; Lynn S. Johnson, "Elizabeth, Bride and Queen," pp.81–83; and Wells, *Spenser's "Faerie Queene"*) — but none has remarked the complete fourfold incestuous aspect of this spousehood.

228. Aristotle, *Politics* 1.12 (Carnes Lord trans., p.52).

229. Thomas Aquinas, *In libros politicorum Aristotelis expositio*, 47f. On this difference see also Marc Shell, *The End of Kinship*, esp. chap.6.

230. See Eduard Eichmann, *Die Kaiserkrönung im Abendland*, 2:94ff. By the same token, calling a person both father and son (as in the *topos* of the *sponsa Christi*), while relatively rare in the early centuries of Christianity, became more common by the twelfth century, thanks partly to the growth of Marian cults. "I am your Father, I am your Son," sang Robert Wace, the Anglo-Norman chronicler of the twelfth century. The material is collected in Anton L. Mayer, "*Mater et filia*"; A. Hahn, *Bibliothek der Symbole*, p.176, 81f; and L. E. Wels, *Theologische Streifzüge*, 1:33–51, who considers the father-son antiphrasis a kind of Sabellianism (see Ernst H. Kantorowicz, *The King's Two Bodies*, pp.99–100).

231. Lucas de Penna, *Commentaria in tres libros Codicis*; Charles de Grassaille, *Regalium Franciae*, I, ius 20, 217.

232. Guy Coquille, *Les Oeuvres*, 1:3232; quoted in William Farr Church, *Constitutional Thought in Sixteenth-Century France*, p.278 n.16.

233. Kantorowicz, *King's Two Bodies*, p.212.

234. Th. Godefroy, *Le Cérémonial de France*, p.348; for earlier such coronations, see E. S. Dewick, ed., *The Coronation Book of Charles V of France*, pp.33, 83.

235. René Choppin, *De Domanio Franciae*, 3.5, p.449 n.6; cited in Kantorowicz, *King's Two Bodies*, p.223.

236. Sir John Fortescue, *De laudibus legum Angliae*, XIII, pp.30, 17. Cf. Cardinal Pole's letter to Henry VIII: "Your whole reasoning comes to this conclusion that you consider the Church a *corpus politicum*" (*Ad Henricum VIII*, cited in Kantorowicz, *King's Two Bodies*, p.229n).

237. The spouse is intragenerational insofar as he or she is, like oneself, the daughter or son of one's parents (in-law), which suggests that marriage is

so egalitarian as to be incestuous. In *the Elementary Structures of Kinship*, p.489, Claude Lévi-Strauss writes: "Marriage is an arbitration between two loves, parental and conjugal. [The two] are both forms of love, and the instant the marriage takes place, considered in isolation, the two meet and merge; *love has filled the ocean*. Their meeting is doubtless merely a prelude to their substitution for one another, the performance of a sort of *chassé-croisé*. But to intersect they must at least momentarily be joined, and it is this which in all social thought makes marriage a sacred mystery. At this moment, all marriage verges on incest." By *chassé-croisé*, Lévi-Strauss suggests a chiasmatic situation of reciprocal and simultaneous exchanges having for their end no result.

238. "Speech to Commons," 1558–59, in Elizabeth, *Public Speaking*, p.117. In response to the House of Commons' urging her in 1559 to marry — because "nothing can be more repugnant to the common good, than to see a Princesse . . . leade a single life, like a Vestal Nunne" — Elizabeth said: "I have made choyce of this kinde of life, which is moste free, and agreeable for such humane affaires as may tend to his [God's] service. . . . To conclude, I am already bound unto an Husband, which is the Kingdome of England. . . . (And therewithall, stretching out her hand, shee shewed them the Ring with which she was given in marriage, and inagurated to her Kingdome, in expresse and solemne terms.) And reproach mee so no more, (quoth shee) that I have no children: for every one of you, and as many are English, are my Children" (William Camden, *Annales*, bk.1, p.16). John King ("Queen Elizabeth I," pp.33–34) points out that the association of the ring with Elizabeth's marriage to England was important as late as her approach to death, when the coronation ring had to be cut off her finger; this was interpreted as a sign of "the coming dissolution of her 'marriage with her kingdome.'"

239. Elizabeth, "Glass," fol.19r–v.

240. Elizabeth, *Letters*, p.47. Sir Henry Sidney had married Mary Dudley (sister of Elizabeth's favorite, the earl of Leicester) and fathered Philip (the poet, statesman, and soldier who later fell out of the queen's favor when he remonstrated against her proposed marriage with the Duc d'Alençon).

241. Sometimes entitled "On Monsieur's Departure" (Elizabeth, *Poems*, p.5), this poem was probably written about Francis, Duc d'Alençon, in 1582 after marriage negotiations had ended. See Roger Pringle, ed., *A Portrait of Queen Elizabeth I*, p.44.

242. Elizabeth, "Speech to Commons," 1558–59, p.117.

243. It is a commonplace in the current literature that "the Reformation had terminated the *cult of Mary* in England; to a significant extent the 'cult of

Elizabeth' replaced it" (Jardine, *Daughters*, 177). But the real issue here involves the extent and precise mode of that transformation. On the cult of Elizabeth as Virgin Queen, though without reference to fourfold kinship, see Louis Adrian Montrose, "Shaping Fantasies," and Winfried Schleiner, "Divina Virago." On visual representations and icons of Elizabeth as the Virgin Mary, see Strong, *Cult*, esp. p.66, on the "Sieve Portrait" of Elizabeth.

244. For the text of John Dowland, the Elizabethan lutist, see F. A. Yates, *Astraea*, p.78.

245. Bertrand de Salignac de la Mothe Fénelon, quoted in Elizabeth, *Sayings*, pp. 61, 68.

246. See Paul Johnson, *Elizabeth I*, pp. 94–95.

247. See Robert Crosse, *The Lover*, sec.ii.

248. Johnson, *Elizabeth I*.

249. Elizabeth, *Letters*, pp.27, 188.

250. Ibid., p.223. Compare her letter of July 1584, written on receipt of the news of the death of Anjou (one of her so-called suitors), to his mother, Catherine de Medici, queen mother of France: "You will find me the faithfulest daughter and sister that ever Princes had."

251. Neville Williams, *Elizabeth, Queen of England*, p.218; OED, s.v. "cummer."

252. Neale, *Elizabeth I and Her Parliaments*, p.109.

253. John Harington, *Letters and Epigrams*, p.96.

254. Compare the view of Pope Nicholas I, who argues that "one ought to treat a godparent like a parent, even though the relationship is spiritual and not one of blood. That there cannot be marriage in these relationships is for the same reason that the Roman law does not allow marriage between those one adopts and one's own children" (*Responses to the Questions of the Bulgars*, sec.2, 15:402).

255. *King Henry the Eighth*, 5.4.9. *Elishabet*, from the name of the priest Aaron's wife (Elisheba, Exod. 6:23) and of Elisabeth, mother of John the Baptist (Luke 1:5), has been interpreted as "God is fullness" "God of the oath," "God's oath," "God is an oath [by which one swears]," and "consecrated to God." Cf. Bale's translation of the term in his "Epistle Dedicatory," fol.9r; and William Gesenius, *A Hebrew and English Lexicon of the Old Testament*, p.45.

256. Shakespeare, *Richard the Third*, 1.3.208.

257. The last scene of *King Henry the Eighth* shows the Duchess of Norfolk and the Marchioness Dorset, the baby princess's two godmothers, sub-

stituting for her biological mother (the absent Anne Bullen, who is barely mentioned); and it shows King Henry VIII, presumably the biological father, asking the godfather, Cranmer, "What is [the infant's] name?" (5.4.9). Elizabeth's verifiable gossipred has replaced her consanguineous family; as Bale would have it, Elizabeth is one of "many noble women, not rising of flesh and blood . . . but of that mighty living spirit of His which vanquisheth death, hell, and the devil" ("Conclusion," fol.46v).

258. Bale, "Epistle Dedicatory," fol.9v: "The spirit of the eternal son of God, Jesus Christ, be always to your excellent grace assistant that ye may send forth more such wholesome fruits of soul and become a *nourishing mother*" (emphasis added). In the *Monument of Matrones* (2в4v), Bentley praises Elizabeth for styling herself "like a loving mother, and a tender nursse, giving my foster-milke, the foode of [God's] word and Gospell aboundantlie to all" (see also King, *Tudor Royal Iconography*, p.255).

259. "Have I conceived all this people? have I begotten them, that thou shouldest say unto me, Carry them in thy bosom, as a nursing father beareth the suckling child, unto the land which thou swarest unto their fathers?" (Num. 11:12).

260. Against this position, Jardine would insist that "Elizabeth I failed to make other than the impact of a *token* woman on the patriarchal attitudes of the early modern period" (*Daughters*, p.195). I should argue, however, that the parentarchy under Elizabeth did not remain as patriarchal as it had been; that it took on and afterward kept certain aspects of matriarchy. But more important, during the Elizabethan period there began a definite undoing of the old parentarchy, whether male or female; the result was the modern English nation-state, which laid the basis for an eventual "liberation" of males and females alike.

261. Josephine Waters Bennet, *"Measure for Measure" as Royal Entertainment*, p.98.

262. Richard Baker, *Chronicle of the Kings of England*, p.155. For James's homosexuality, see Bennet, *"Measure for Measure" as Royal Entertainment*, p.180 n.39.

263. James I, *Political Works*, pp.272, 24; cited in Jonathan Goldberg, *James I and the Politics of Liberature*, pp.141–42; cf. Leonard Tennenhouse, "Representing Power," p.153.

264. See Perrens, *Les Libertins*.

265. James Otis, quoted in Samuel Eliot Morison, *The Oxford History of the American People*, p.205.

266. So sang the rock-and-roll group The Animals in San Francisco's spectacular Cow Palace in 1966. Cf. "Therefore shall a man leave his father and his mother" (Gen. 2:24).

JOHN BALE: EDITOR'S FOREWORD

1. For the various complications, see E. K. Chambers, "Geoffrey of Monmouth and the *Brut.*" See also Hugh A. MacDougall, *Racial Myth in English History*, from which many references in this section are taken.

2. Halvdan Koht, "The Dawn of Nationalism in Europe," p.271.

3. Geoffrey of Monmouth, *The History of the Kings of Britain*, p.107.

4. Bernardus Andreas, *Historia Regis Henrici Septimi*, pp.9–11.

5. See Sydney Anglo, "British History in Early Tudor Propaganda."

6. Cited in John Speed, *The History of Great Britain*, p.164.

7. R. Kroebner, "The Imperial Crown of This Realm," p.40.

8. Ibid., p.31.

9. On *sang real*, see Marc Shell, *Money, Language, and Thought*, chap.2.

10. Sharon Turner, *History of the Anglo-Saxons*, 3:488–89, says that "the Anglo-Saxon church formed a remarkable contrast to the Roman hierarchy of subsequent ages" and stresses that transubstantiation was not a doctrine. As Saint Hilda pointed out at Whitby in 664, in Celtic Christianity the tonsure was different, for example, and so was the celebration time of Easter.

11. This is not Saint Augustine of Hippo, author of the great *Confessions*, but the Roman missionary who became the first archbishop of Canterbury.

12. C. E. Wright, "The Dispersal of Monastic Libraries."

13. John Bale, *Select Works*, p.188.

14. Joscelyn's edition of Gildas appeared in 1568.

15. Denys Hay, *Polydore Vergil.*

16. Richard Verstegen, *A Restitution of Decayed Intelligence in Antiquities*, p.203–4, called the Danes and the English one tribe: "And whereas some do call us a mixed Nation by reasons of these Danes and Normans coming in among us, I answer, as formerly I have noted, that the Danes and the Normans were once the same people with the Germans, as were also the Saxons; and we are not to be accompted mixed by having only some such joined onto us again, as sometime had one same language, and one same origin with us." Shakespeare's Hamlet (or "Brutus") is discussed in these geopolitical terms in my forthcoming *Children of the Earth*, chap.3.

17. John Rastell, *The Pastyme of People*, p.7.

18. See John Leland, *Assertio inclytissimii Arturii.*

19. Tacitus writes: "I accept the view that the peoples of Germany have never been tainted by intermarriage with other peoples, and stand out as a nation peculiar, pure, and unique of its kind" (*Tacitus on Britain and Germany*, p.103). John Hare, *St. Edward's Ghost*, pp.3–4, represents one early (1640s) zenith in this British-Teutonic racialist tradition: "To the Antiquity of the Teutonic house, there wants not a conspiring quality of blood effectual to make it the most illustrious and primer Nation of Christendome."

20. William Camden made this a gist of his *Britannia* (1586).

21. Luther, "An Appeal to . . . the Ruling Class of German Nationality," pp.192–93.

22. Constantine the Great was the illegitimate son of Flavius Valerius Constantius. Constantius, later Emperor Constantius I (called "Chlorus"), reestablished Roman power in Britain, ruled as Caesar in 305–6 A.D., and died in York. Constantius had been adopted and appointed Caesar by Emperor Maximian I (ruled 286–305 and 306–8), whose stepdaughter, Flavia Maximiana Theodora Constantinus, he married in 289 A.D. after renouncing his first wife Helena. Constantine claimed legal right to the Empire of the West in about 310 A.D., but because his claim rested mainly on his recognition by the then defeated and disgraced Maximian I, he had to find additional grounds to support his claim. One such was the assertion of a fictitious connection between his father, Constantius Chlorus, and the family of Claudius Gothicus: he misrepresented Claudius Gothicus as the father — instead of the nephew — of Constantius Chlorus. See EB, s.v. "Constantine," p.988.

23. Cited in Leon Poliakov, *The Aryan Myth*, p.82.

24. Speed, *History of Great Britain*, pp.287–89.

25. Consider the Emperor (*basileus*) Irene in the Eastern Roman Empire in the eighth century (regent during the minority of Constantine VI), the Hungarian King Maria in the fourteenth century, and the Hungarian Emperor Maria Theresa in the eighteenth century; cf. Kantorowicz, *King's Two Bodies*, p.80.

26. The "Epistle Dedicatory" and "Conclusion" are transcribed here, with some modernization, from Bale's 1548 edition of Elizabeth's "Glass" — *A Godly Medytacyon of the Christen Sowle* — as are the "Four Sentences" translated by Elizabeth from the apocryphal book of Ecclesiasticus. For identification of allusions, see the Glossary of Proper Names in Bale, below. Sources used for the Glossary include Bale's own indexes, as well as works by Ponticus Virrunius, Geoffrey of Monmouth, and Raphael Holinshed. Because medieval

historiography was hardly scientific, I do not distinguish between fact and fiction.

1. Salminen, in *Miroir*, p.257, remarks that the text was manipulated, probably by Catherine Parr (perhaps with Elizabeth), and later certainly by John Bale.

2. One reason (besides fear of politically motivated censorship) that many English writers of the period, Bale among them, chose to publish their English works in Germany was the reputation of the German presses for greater accuracy. English compositors and publishing houses frequently committed the "errors" to which scribes are generally liable — misreading, eyeskip, dittography, haplography, transposition sophistication, substitution, simple omission, simple interpolation — as well as those errors specific to the medium of print (cf. Gary Taylor, "General Introduction" to *The Complete Oxford Shakespeare*, pp.43–45, 21–23).

3. The editions of James Cancellar contain interesting material — including a seven-page "Dedication" in which he praises the learning of Princess Elizabeth and the virtue of virginity — but they are truncated and unpredictable. Cancellar's claim that in his edition "the corruption & faultes of the olde print [are] corrected and amended" is too self-serving to be trusted. And R. B. McKerrow (*Dictionary of Printers and Booksellers*, pp.282–83) points out that Roger Ward had an especially poor reputation.

4. Roger Ward does not include the Four Sentences.

5. Because the original manuscript is listed in early bibliographies and has been known to antiquarians for centuries, current editorial interest in the "fiction" of an original, ideal, or *authentic* text (as is generally lacking in the preeminent case of Shakespeare) is not, strictly speaking, relevant here. Nor is the usual interest in canon formation as cultural symptom (which edition of *King Lear* is paramount? why is one edition popular in one period and another in a different period?); it applies only insofar as we address the traditional canon's exclusion of the "Glass" (see my Introduction).

6. For a general introduction to the problem of orthography, see Stanley Wells, *Modernizing Shakespeare's Spelling*. For a transcription and remarks on particular problems of orthography, see Salminen's edition of the *Miroir*.

7. OED, s.v. "Collation," 3.

8. Taylor, "General Introduction," p.60.

9. For some of the following remarks I am indebted both to Prescott, "Pearl," esp. pp.68–70; and Salminen, *Miroir*, esp. 264–85.

10. E.g., *ardeur* becomes "goodness."

11. E.g., Elizabeth refuses to call herself "Chienne morte, pourriture de siens" (Marguerite, *Miroir*, line 1374).

12. For example, "O Mort, O Mort" (ibid., line 1109) becomes "Death" (Elizabeth, "Glass," fol.50r).

13. Marguerite, *Miroir*, lines 587–88; Elizabeth, "Glass," fol.30r.

14. Salminen, *Miroir*, p.279, notes their frequency but adds that it is not useful to prolong the list of such "errors."

15. *Miroir*, lines 581–84; "Glass," fol.29v.

16. *Miroir*, line 468; "Glass," fol.25r, before "O sweet Jesus."

17. *Miroir*, lines 350–52; "Glass," fol.20v.

18. *Miroir*, line 633; "Glass," fol.32r (emphasis added). The apparent confusion of *father* with *mother* is not related to the gender-based character of French grammar, though it is worth noting that personal pronouns and nouns *are* gendered in French: *âme* (soul), for example, is always feminine.

19. See Joseph L. Allaire, Introduction (p.22) to his edition of Marguerite's *Miroir*; and Salminen, *Miroir*, p.38.

20. Anne, for example, supported the 1536 reprint of Tyndale's New Testament and gave her serving women miniature psalters and biblical prayer books (Ives, *Anne Boleyn*, p.315).

Bibliography of Works Cited

ABBREVIATIONS

CC   *Corpus Christianorum* (*Series Latina*). Turnhout, Belgium, 1953–.

CSEL   *Corpus scriptorium ecclesiasticorum latinorum.* Vienna, 1866– .

GCS   *Die griechischen christlichen Schriftsteller der ersten drei Jahrhunderte.* Leipzig, 1897–1909.

EB   *Encyclopedia Britannica.* 11th ed. 32 vols. New York, 1910–11.

EETS   Early English Text Society.

Harl   Harleian manuscript (British Library).

LP   *Letters and Papers, Foreign and Domestic, of the Reign of Henry VIII, 1509–1547.* Ed. James Gairdner and R. H. Brodie. 21 vols. London, 1862–1910.

LW   *Luther's Works.* Ed. Jaroslav Pelikan and Helmut T. Lehmann. 55 vols. Philadelphia, 1960–62.

OED   *Oxford English Dictionary.* 12 vols. Oxford, 1933.

PG   *Patrologiae cursus completus* (*Series Graeca*). Ed. J. P. Migne. 161 vols. Paris, 1857–99.

PL   *Patrologiae cursus completus* (*Series Latina*). Ed. J. P. Migne. 221 vols. Paris, 1844–64.

Works Cited

Acta sanctorum. Ed. and pub. Society of the Bollandists. 67 vols. Brussels, 1863.

Aelred of Rievaulx. *De vita eremitica*. Ed. Carl Horstmann. *Englische Studien* 7 (1884): 304–44.

Allo, E.-B. *Saint Paul: Première epitre aux Corinthiens*. Paris, 1956.

Ames, Percy W. Introduction. In Elizabeth, *The Mirror of the Sinful Soul* (facsimile), ed. Percy W. Ames. London, 1897.

Ancrene Riwle. In Kurath, Kuhn, and Reidy, *Middle English Dictionary*, Ann Arbor, Mich., 1956– .

Andreas, Bernardus. *Historia Regis Henrici Septimi*. In *Memorials of Henry VII*, ed. James Gairdner. London, 1858.

Anglo, Sydney. "The British History in Early Tudor Propaganda." *Bulletin of the Johns Rylands Library* 44 (1961–62): 21–44.

Animals, The. "We Gotta Get Out of This Place." MGM 13382, single, 45 RPM.

Aquinas, Thomas. *In libros politicorum Aristotelis expositio*. Ed. R. M. Spiazzi. Turin, 1951.

———. *Summa contra gentiles*. Trans. English Dominican Fathers. 2 vols. New York, 1924.

———. *Summa theologica*. Trans. Fathers of the English Dominican Province. 3 vols. New York, 1947.

Aristotle. *Politics*. Trans. H. Rackham. Cambridge, Mass., 1967.

———. *Politics*. Trans. Carnes Lord. Chicago, 1984.

Ascham, Roger. *The Scholemaster*. London, 1570.

Ascoli, G. *La Grande-Bretagne devant l'opinion française*. Paris, 1927.

Askew, Anne. *The First Examinacyon of Anne Askewe . . . with the Elucydacyon of Johan Bale*. Wesel, 1546.

———. *The Lattre Examinacyon of Anne Askewe . . . with the Elucydacyon of Johan Bale*. Wesel, 1547.

Athanasius?. *Vita Antonii*. In *Vita patrum*, ed. H. Rosweyd. PL 73:117–91.

Bibliography of Works Cited

Awdelay, John. *The Fraternitie of Vacabondes* (1565). EETS, ext. ser. no.5. London, 1869.

Bainton, Roland. *Women of the Reformation: In France and England.* Boston, 1975.

Baker, Richard. *Chronicle of the Kings of England.* London, 1643.

Bakhtin, Mikhail. *Rabelais and His World.* Trans. Helene Iswolsky. Cambridge, Mass., 1968.

Balbus, Bernardus [Bishop of Faenza and Pavia]. *Summa decretalium.* Ed. E. A. T. Laspeyres. Ratisbon, 1860.

Bale, John. *A Brief Chronicle concerning the Examination and Death of Sir John Oldcastle, Collected by John Bale out of the Books and Writings of Those Popish Prelates Which Were Present.* London, 1544.

———. *Complete Plays of John Bale.* Ed. Peter Happé. 2 vols. Cambridge, 1985–86.

———. "Epistle Dedicatory" and "Conclusion." In Elizabeth I, *A Godly Medytacyon of the Christian Sowle.* 1548, 1590.

———. *Illustrium majoris Britanniae scriptorum, hoc est, Angliae, Cambriae, ac Scotiae summarium.* Ipswich and Wesel, 1548, 1549.

———. *The Image of Both Churches.* Ed. Henry Christmas. In Bale, *Select Works.*

———. *Index Britanniae scriptorum quos . . . collegit Ionnes Baleum.* Ed. R. Lane Poole with Mary Bateson. Oxford, 1902.

———. *Kynge Johan.* Ed. J. P. Collier. Camden Society. London, 1838.

———. *Scriptorum illustrium majoris Britanniae . . . catalogus.* Rewritten version of Bale, *Illustrium.* Basel, 1557–79.

———. *Select Works.* Ed. Henry Christmas. 1849; New York, 1968.

———. *The Three Laws of Nature.* London, 1908.

———. *Vocacyon of Johan Bale.* Eds. John N. King and Peter Happé. Renaissance English Text Society. Binghampton, N.Y., 1990.

———, ed. John Lambert, *A Treatyse Made by Johan Lambert vnto Kynge Henry the VIII concernynge His Opynyon in the Sacrament of the Altar.* 1538; Wesel, 1548 (?).

——, ed. John Leland. *The Laboryouse Journey & Serche . . . for En-glandes Antiquitees, Geuven of Hym as a New Yeares Gyfte to Kynge Henry the VIII . . . with Declaracyons Enlarged.* London, 1549 (?).

——, trans. Jonas Justus, *The Trye Hystorie of the Christen Departynge of Martyne Luther.* Wesel, 1546.

Bandinelli, Orlando [Alexander III]. *Summa.* Ed. Friedrich Thaner. Innsbruck, 1874.

Bayle, Pierre. *Dictionnaire historique et critique.* Rev. ed. 16 vols. Paris, 1820–24.

Bede. *History of the Church of England (Historia ecclesiastica gentis Anglo-rum).* Trans. T. Stapleton. Antwerp, 1565.

Bédier, Joseph. "La Tradition manuscrite du *Lai de l'Ombre.*" *Romania* 54 (1928): 161–96, 321–56.

Bernardete, Seth. "A Reading of Sophocles' *Antigone.*" *Interpretation* 4, no.3 (1975): 148–96; 5, nos.1–2 (1975): 1–56, 148–84.

Bennet, Josephine Waters. *"Measure for Measure" as Royal Entertainment.* New York, 1966.

Benrath, Karl. *Bernardino Ochino von Siena: Ein Beitrag zur Geschichte der Reformation.* 1892; Nieuwkoop, 1968.

Bentley, Thomas, ed. *Monument of Matrones: Containing Seven Lamps of Virginite.* Vol. 1. London, 1582.

Bernard of Clairvaux. *On the Song of Songs.* Trans. Kilian Walsh, intro. M. Corneille Halflants. Cistercian Fathers ser. 4, 7, 31, 40. In *The Works of Bernard of Clairvaux*, vols. 2–5. Spencer, Mass., 1970.

Bernardine of Siena. *Opera omnia.* Florence, 1950–56.

Bernardo, Reta Mohney. "The Problem of Perspective in the *Miroir de l'âme pecheresse*, the *Prisons*, and the *Heptameron* of Marguerite de Navarre." Ph.D. diss., State University of New York (Binghamton), 1979.

Bible.

Le *Nouveau Testament* (1523). Trans. Jacques Lefèvre d'Etaples. Mouton, 1970.

The Tyndale New Testament. 1534.

The Coverdale Bible. 1535.

The Great Bible. 1539.

The Geneva Bible (1560). Ed. Lloyd E. Berry. Madison, Wis., 1969.

The King James (Authorized) Version. 1611.

The Twenty-Four Books of the Old Testament. Hebrew and English text, trans. Alexander Harkavy. 4 vols. New York, 1928.

Novum Testamentum Graece et Latine. Ed. August Merck. 6th ed. Rome, 1948.

Blackmore, Simon Augustine. "Hamlet's Right to the Crown." In *The Riddles of Hamlet and the Newest Answers.* Boston, 1917.

Blake, William. *The Complete Writings.* Ed. G. Keynes. London, 1957.

Bonaventure [Giovanni di Fidanza]. *The Soul's Journey into God, the Tree of Life, and the Life of Saint Francis.* Trans. Ewert Cousins. New York, 1978.

Bradbrook, Muriel C. "Virtue Is the True Nobility." *Review of English Studies,* n.s. 1 (1950): 289–301.

Brain, Robert. *Friends and Lovers.* New York, 1976.

Brântome, Pierre de Bourdeille. *Les Dames galantes.* Ed. Maurice Rat. Paris, 1960.

Brown, Norman O. *Love's Body.* New York, 1966.

Bugge, John. *Virginitas: An Essay in the History of a Medieval Ideal.* The Hague, 1975.

Calendars of Letters, Despatches, and State Papers relating to the Negotiations between England and Spain. Ed. G. A. Bergenroth et al. London, 1862–1954.

Calo, Jeanne, *La création de la femme chez Michelet.* Paris, 1975.

Calvin, John. *Opera omnia.* Ed. J. W. Baum, E. Cunitz, E. Reuss, P. Lobstein, and A. Erichson. 59 vols. Berlin, 1863–1900.

Camden, William. *Annales: The True and Royall History of the Famous Empress Elizabeth, Queen of England, France, and Ireland, etc.* 1625.

———. *Britannia.* London, 1586.

Bibliography of Works Cited

Campbell, P. G. C. "Christine de Pisan en Angleterre." *Revue de littérature comparée* (Paris) 1926:659–70.

Carlyle, Thomas. *Oliver Cromwell's Letters and Speeches.* London, 1845.

Cazauran, Nicole. "La Trentième Nouvelle de l'*Heptameron* ou la méditation d'un 'Exemple.'" In *Mélanges Jeanne Lods*, pp.617–52. Paris, 1978.

Chambers, E. K. "Geoffrey of Monmouth and the *Brut* as Sources of Early English History." *History* 3 (1918–19): 225–28.

Chambers, R. W. *Thomas More.* New York, 1936.

Champneys, John. *The Harvest Is at Hand. . . .* London, 1548.

Chapman, George. *Chapman's Homer: The 'Iliad,' The 'Odyssey,' and the 'Lesser Homerica.'* Ed. Allardyce Nicoll. Princeton, 1967.

Charles de Grassaille. *Regalium Franciae libri duo.* Paris, 1545.

Chaucer, Geoffrey. "The Parson's Prologue and Tale (exclusive of the Retraction)." In *The Text of the Canterbury Tales*, ed. John M. Manly and Edith Rickert, 4:361–476. Chicago, 1940.

———. *The Riverside Chaucer.* 3d ed. Ed. Larry D. Benson. (Based on *The Works of Geoffrey Chaucer*, ed. F. N. Robinson, 1957.) Boston, 1987.

Cherry, C. L. *The Most Unvaluedst Purchase: Women in the Plays of Thomas Middleton.* Salzburg, 1973.

Cholakian, Patricia Francis. *Rape and Writing in the "Heptameron" of Marguerite de Navarre.* Carbondale, Ill., 1991.

Choppin, René. *De domanio Franciae.* Paris, 1605.

Christine de Pizan. *The Book of the City of Ladies.* Trans. Earl Jeffrey Richards. New York, 1982.

Church, William Farr. *Constitutional Thought in Sixteenth-Century France.* Harvard Historical Studies 47. Cambridge, Mass., 1941.

Clement of Alexandria. *Stromata.* Ed. Otto Stahlin. In GCS 3:6.

Clement [Pseudo-]. *Epistolae ad virgines.* PG 1:379–416.

Cohn, Norman. "The Cult of the Free Spirit: A Medieval Heresy Reconstructed." *Psychoanalysis and the Psychoanalytic Review* 48 (1961): 51–68.

Collins, Adela Yarbro. "The Function of 'Excommunication' in Paul." *Harvard Theological Review* 73 (1980): 251–63.

Collins, Joseph B. *Christian Mysticism in the Elizabethan Age*. Baltimore, Md., 1940.

Conzelmann, Hans. *1 Corinthians*. Philadelphia, 1975.

Cooper, J. M. "Incest Prohibitions in Primitive Culture." *Ecclesiastical Review* 33 (1932): 4–7.

Coquille, Guy. *Les Oeuvres*. 2 vols. Paris, 1666.

Cousins, Ewert H. *Bonaventure and the Coincidence of Opposites*. Chicago, 1978.

Cranenburgh, H. van. "De teksten van Hadewijch over het delen in Maria's goddelijk moederschap" [on spiritual maternity]. *Ons Geestelijk Erf* 33 (1959): 377–405.

———. "Hadewychs twaalfde visioen en negende stophisch gedicht" [on spousal mysticism]. *Ons Geestelijk Erf* 35 (1961): 361–84.

Craster, H. H. E. "An Unknown Translation by Queen Elizabeth." *English Historical Review* 29 (1914): 721–23.

Cronica del Rey Henrico Otavo de Inglaterra. Ed. Marquis de Molins. Madrid, 1874. Trans. as *Chronicle of King Henry VIII of England*, ed. M. A. S. Hume. London, 1889.

Crosse, Robert. *The Lover; or, Nuptial Love*. London, 1638.

Curtius, Ernst Robert. *European Literature and the Latin Middle Ages*. Trans. Willard R. Trask. New York, 1953.

Dagens, Jean. "Le *Miroir des simple ames* et Marguerite de Navarre." In *La mystique Rhénane: Colloque de Strasbourg 16–19 mai 1961*, pp.281–89. Paris, 1963.

Damasus. *Epigrammata*. Ed. and trans. Antonius Ferrua. The Vatican, 1942.

Dareste de la Chavanne [Antoine Elisabeth Cléophas]. *Histoire de France depuis les origines jusqu'à nos jours*. 3d. ed. 9 vols. Paris, 1884–85.

Del Mar, Alexander. *Ancient Britain in the Light of Modern Archaeological Discoveries.* New York, 1900.

De Quincey, Thomas. *Selections Grave and Gay: Writings Published and Unpublished.* 14 vols. Edinburgh, 1853–60.

Dewhurst, J. "The Alleged Miscarriages of Catherine of Aragon and Anne Boleyn." *Medical History* 28 (1984): 49–56.

Dewick, E. S., ed. *The Coronation Book of Charles V. of France.* Bradshaw Society, XVI. London, 1899.

Dionysius Carthusianus [Denis de Leewis]. *The Mirroure of Golde for the Synfull Soule.* Trans. Margaret, Countess of Richmond. London, 1522.

Doiron, Marilyn. "The Middle English Translation of *Le Mirouer des simples ames.*" In *Dr. L. Reypens-Album,* ed. L. Reypens and Alb. Ampe, pp.131–51. Antwerp, 1964.

Döllinger, I. I. von. *Beiträge zur Sektengeschichte des Mittelalters.* 2 pts. Munich, 1890.

Dowling, Maria. "Anne Boleyn and Reform." *Journal of Ecclesiastical History* 35 (1984): 30–46.

Duff, I. F. Grant. "Die Beziehung Elizabeth-Essex: Eine psychoanalytische Betrachtung." *Psychoanalytische Bewegung* 3 (1931): 457–74.

Dumm, Demetrius. *The Theological Basis of Virginity according to Saint Jerome.* Latrobe, Pa., 1961.

Ecclesiasticus (The Wisdom of Jeshua, the Son of Sirach). In *The Apocrypha: An American Translation,* trans. Edgar Goodspeed, pp.221–328. Chicago, 1938.

Eekhoud, G. *Les libertins d'Anvers: Legendes et histoire des Loisistes.* Paris, 1912.

Egido, Téofanes. "The Historical Setting of St. Teresa's Life." *Carmelite Studies,* 1980.

Eichmann, Eduard. *Die Kaisarkrönung im Abendland.* 2 vols. Oxford, 1921.

Elizabeth I. *Englishings of Boethius, De Consolatione Philosophiae, A.D. 1593; Plutarch, De Curiositate, A.D. 1598; and Horace, De Arte Poetica (part), 1598.* Ed. Caroline Pemberton. EETS, orig. ser. 113. London, 1899.

———. "The Glass of the Sinful Soul" (1544). Bodleian Library, Oxford. Cherry 36. (Description: see Madan, *A Summary Catalogue of Western Manuscripts*, no.9810. Facsimile: see Ames, *The Mirror of the Sinful Soul.* Transcription: see Salminen, *Le Miroir de l'âme pécheresse.*)

———. *A Godly Medytacyon of the Christen Sowle, concerning a Love Towardes God and His Christe, Compiled in French by Lady Margarete Quene of Nauerre, and Aptely Translated into English by the Ryght Vertuouse Lady Elyzabeth Daughter to Our Late Soverayne King Henry the VIII.* Ed. (with dedication and conclusion) John Bale; printed by Dirik van der Straten. Marburg, 1548. Subsequent editions: ed. (with introduction) James Cancellar (London, 1568); ed. (with introduction and dedication) James Cancellar (London, 1582); as "Lamp 2" in Bentley, *Monument of Matrones* (London, 1582); ed. Roger Ward (London, 1590).

———. *Letters of Queen Elizabeth.* Ed. G. B. Harrison. London, 1935.

———. *Poems of Queen Elizabeth I.* Ed. Leicester Bradner. Providence, R.I., 1964.

———. *The Public Speaking of Queen Elizabeth.* Ed. George P. Rice. New York, 1951.

———. *The Sayings of Queen Elizabeth.* Ed. Frederick Chamberlain. London, 1923.

———. Texts embroidered on black cloth covers of sextodecimo New Testament containing part of Laurence Tomson's *New Testament* (1578). Bodl. MS e. Mus. 242.

———. Translation (English) of John Calvin's *Institution Chrétienne.* MS, Scottish Record Office.

———. Translation (Latin) of Bernardino Ochino's *De Christo sermo.* MS Bodley 6.

335

Bibliography of Works Cited

——. Translations (Latin, French, Italian) of Catherine Parr's *Prayers, or Meditations,* titled "Precationes sev meditationes." British Library, MS Royal 7 D. X. MS. 1545.

Elyot, Thomas. *The Image of Governaunce Compiled by the Actes and Sentences Notable of the Most Noble Emperor Alexandre Seuerus.* London, 1544.

Encyclopaedia of Islam. 2d ed. 7 vols. Leiden, 1960– .

Erbstösser, M., and E. Werner. *Ideologische Probleme de.s mittelalterischen Pleberjetums: Die freigeistige Häresie und ihr sozialen Wurzeln.* Berlin, 1960.

Eusebius Pamphili of Caesarea. *The History of the Church from Christ to Constantine.* Trans. G. A. Williamson. New York, 1966.

Fairfield, Leslie P. *John Bale: Mythmaker for the English Reformation.* West Lafayette, Ind., 1976.

Farr, Edward, ed. *Selected Poetry, Chiefly Devotional, of the Reign of Queen Elizabeth.* 2 pts. Parker Society. Cambridge, 1845.

Feije, H. *De impedimentis et dispensationibus matrimonialibus.* Louvain, 1885.

Filmer, Robert. *Partriarcha and Other Political Works.* Ed. Peter Laslett. Oxford, 1949.

Fortescue, Sir John. *De laudibus legum Angliae.* Ed. S. B. Chrimes. Oxford, 1885.

Fowler, John Howard. "The Development of Incest Regulations in the Early Middle Ages: Family, Nurturance, and Aggression in the Making of the Medieval West." Ph.D. diss., Rice University, 1981.

Foxe, John. *Actes and Monuments of These Latter and Perillous Dayes* [The Book of Martyrs]. London, 1563.

Fraenger, Wilhelm. *The Millennium of Hieronymus Bosch: Outlines of a New Interpretation.* Trans. Eithne Wilkins and Ernst Kaiser. London, 1952.

Francis of Assisi. *Gli scritti di San Francesco d'Assisi.* Milan, 1954.

——. *Saint Francis: Omnibus of Sources.* Ed. Marion A. Habig. Chicago, 1973.

Bibliography of Works Cited

Frederichs, J. "Un Luthérien français devenu libertin spirituel: Christophe Hérault et les Loisistes d'Anvers (1490–1544)." *Bulletin de la Société de l'Histoire du Protestantisme Français* 41 (1892): 250–69.

Freud, Sigmund. *Civilization and Its Discontents.* Trans. James Strachey. New York, 1962.

——. "Obsessive Acts and Religious Practices." In *Collected Papers*, ed. Ernest Jones, 2:25–35. New York, 1959.

——. "The Taboo on Virginity." In *Standard Edition of the Complete Psychological Works of Sigmund Freud*, ed. James Strachey with Anna Freud, 11:191–208. London, 1953–66.

——. *Totem and Taboo.* Trans. James Strachey. New York, 1950.

Friedman, Albert B. " 'When Adam Delved . . .': Contexts of a Historic Proverb." In *The Learned and the Lewed: Studies in Chaucer and Medieval Literature*, ed. Larry D. Benson. Harvard English Studies 5. Cambridge, Mass., 1974.

Friedmann, Paul. *Anne Boleyn: A Chapter of English History, 1527–1536.* 2 vols. London, 1884; New York, 1973.

Gardiner, Samuel Rawson. *History of the Great Civil War, 1642–1649.* 4 vols. London, 1886–91.

Gardiner, Stephen. *Letters.* New York, 1933.

Gartenberg, P. and N. Thames Whittemore, "A Checklist of English Women in Print, 1475–1640." *Bulletin of Bibliography* 34 (1977): 1–13.

Gellius, Aulus. *Les nuits attiques.* Ed. René Marache. Paris, 1967.

Génin, François. *Nouvelles Lettres de la reine de Navarre adressés au roi François Ier son frère.* Paris, 1842.

Geoffrey of Monmouth. *Historia Regum Britanniae.* Ed. Ivo Cavellatus. Paris, 1508, 1517.

——. *The History of the Kings of Britain.* Trans. Lewis Thorpe. Harmondsworth, 1966.

Gesenius, William. *A Hebrew and English Lexicon of the Old Testament.* Trans. Edward Robinson, ed. Francis Brown. Oxford, 1972.

Gildas. *De excidio et conquestu Britanniae.* Ed. J. Joscelyn (Josselinus). London, 1568. (Also ed. P. Vergilius and R. Ridley, London, 1525.)

A Glasse of the Truthe. Dialogue between a lawyer and a divine concerning the king's proposed divorce, attributed to Henry VIII. London, 1532.

Godefroy, Théodore. *Le Cérémonial de France.* Paris, 1619.

Goldberg, Jonathan. *James I and the Politics of Literature: Jonson, Shakespeare, Donne, and Their Contemporaries.* Baltimore, Md., 1983.

Gower, John. *Confessio amantis,* vols. 2–3 of *The Complete Works of John Gower.* Ed. G. C. M. Macaulay. London, 1901.

Grandes Chroniques de France. Ed. Jules Edouard M. Viard. Paris, 1920–53.

Gratian. *Decretum (Concordia discordantium canorum).* Ed. A. L. Richter, rev. A. Friedberg. In *Corpus iuris canonici,* vol. 1. Leipzig, 1879.

Gregory of Nyssa. *Vita S. Macrinae.* PG 46:959–99.

Gregory the Great. *Vita S. Benedicti.* PL 66:125–215.

Guarnieri, Romana. *Il movimento dei libero spirito: Testi e documenti.* Rome, 1965. (Reissue of *Archivio Italiano per la storia della pieto* 4 [1964]: 353–708.)

Hadewijch. *De Visioenen.* Ed. Josef van Mierlo. Louvain, 1924–25.

Hahn, A. *Bibliothek der Symbole und Glaubensregln der alten Kirche.* 2d ed. Breslau, 1877.

Halley, Janet E. "Heresy, Orthodoxy, and the Politics of Religious Discourse: The Case of the English Family of Love." *Representations* 15 (1986): 98–120.

Hamilton, John. *The Catechism.* 1552; London, 1884.

Hannay, Margaret P., ed. *Silent but for the Word: Tudor Women as Patrons, Translators, and Writers of Religious Works.* Kent, Ohio, 1985.

Harding, Mary Esther. *Woman's Mysteries, Ancient and Modern.* London, 1935.

Hare, John. *St. Edward's Ghost; or, anti-Normanisme, Being a Pathetical Complaint and Motion in the Behalfe of Our English Nation against her Grand (yet Neglected) Grievance, Normanisme.* London, 1647.

her Grand (yet Neglected) Grievance, Normanisme. London, 1647.

Harington, John. *Letters and Epigrams.* Ed. N. E. McClure. Philadelphia, 1930.

The Harleian Miscellany. Ed. William Oldys and Thomas Park. 10 vols. London, 1808–13.

Harney, Martin P. *Brother and Sister Saints.* Paterson, N.J., 1957.

Harris, Jesse W. *John Bale: A Study in the Minor Literature of the Reformation.* Urbana, Ill., 1940.

Hartmann von Aue. *Gregorius: A Medieval Oedipus Legend.* Trans. Edwin H. Zeydel. Chapel Hill, N.C., 1955.

Haugaard, William P. "Elizabeth Tudor's *Book of Devotions*: A Neglected Clue to the Queen's Life and Character." *Sixteenth Century Journal* 12, no.2 (1981): 79–106.

Hauser, Henri. *Etudes sur la reforme française.* Paris, 1909.

Hay, Denys. *Polydore Vergil.* Oxford, 1952.

Hefele, Carl Joseph von. *Conciliengeschichte.* 9 vols. Freiburg, 1855–87.

Hegel, Georg Wilhelm Friedrich. *Werke.* 20 vols. Frankfurt, 1969–71.

Hexter, J. H. *More's Utopia: The Biography of an Idea.* New York, 1965.

Histoire de Anne Boleyne Jadis Royne d'Angeterre. 1545.

Holinshed, Raphael. *The Chronicles of England, Scotland, and Ireland.* 6 vols. London, 1807–8.

Hughey, Ruth. "A Note on Queen Elizabeth's 'Godly Meditation.'" *The Library*, 4th ser. 25 (1935): 237–40.

Ignatius of Antioch. "The Epistle of the Ephesians." In *Corpus Ignatium: A Complete Collection of the Ignatian Epistles*, ed. William Cureton, pp.15–38. Berlin, 1849. (Also in PG 5:729–56.)

Ives, Eric. *Anne Boleyn.* Oxford, 1986.

Bibliography of Works Cited

Jacob's Well: An English Treatise on the Cleansing of Man's Conscience. Ed. Arthur Brandeis. EETS, old ser. London, 1900.

James I [James VI of Scotland]. *The Political Works of James I.* Ed. Charles Howard McIlwain. Cambridge, Mass., 1918.

Jardine, Alice A. *Gynesis: Configurations of Women and Modernity.* Ithaca, N.Y., 1985.

Jardine, Lisa. *"Still Harping on Daughters": Women and Drama in the Age of Shakespeare.* 2d ed. New York, 1989.

Jerome. *Epistulae.* Ed. Isidorus Hilberg. In CSEL 54–56.

John Chrysostom. *De virginitate.* PG 48:533–96.

John of the Cross. *The Collected Works of St. John of the Cross.* Trans. Kieran Kavanaugh and Otilio Rodriguez. Washington, D.C., 1973.

Johnson, Lynn Stanley. "Elizabeth, Bride and Queen: A Study of Spenser's April Eclogue and the Metaphors of English Protestantism." *Spenser Studies* 2 (1981): 75–81.

Johnson, Paul. *Elizabeth I: A Study in Power and Intellect.* London, 1974.

Jonas of Orleans. *De institutione laicali.* PL 106:122–278.

Jones, Ernst. *Hamlet and Oedipus.* New York, 1976.

Jordan, Constance. "Feminism and the Humanists: The Case of Sir Thomas Elyot's *Defence of Good Women.*" *Renaissance Quarterly* 36, no.2 (1983): 181–201.

Julian of Norwich. *Revelations of Divine Love.* Ed. Grace Warrack. 3d ed. London, 1950.

Julius I. *Decreta julii papae decem.* PL 8:967–71.

Justinian the Great. *Dialogue with Tryphon.* PG 6:471–800.

Kantorowicz, Ernst H. *The King's Two Bodies: A Study in Medieval Political Theology.* Princeton, N.J., 1957.

Kaula, David. *Shakespeare and the Archpriest Controversy: A Study of Some New Sources.* The Hague, 1975.

Kelly, J. Thomas. *Thorn on the Tudor Rose: Monks, Rogues, Vagabonds, and Sturdy Beggars.* Jackson, Miss., 1977.

Kelly-Gadol, Joan. "Did Women Have a Renaissance?" In *Becoming Visible: Women in European History*, ed. Renate Bridenthal and Claudia Koonz, pp.137–64. Boston, 1977.

Kelso, R. *Doctrine of the Lady of the Renaissance*. Urbana, Ill., 1956.

Kennard, Joseph Spencer. *The Friar in Fiction, Sincerity in Art, and Other Essays*. New York, 1923.

Kersey, John. *Dictionarium Anglo-britannicum; or, A General English Dictionary* (1708). 3d ed. London, 1721.

King, John N. *English Reformation Literature: The Tudor Origin of the Protestant Tradition*. Princeton, N.J., 1982.

——. "Patronage and Piety: The Influence of Catherine Parr." In Hannay, *Silent but for the Word*, pp.264–66.

——. "Queen Elizabeth I: Representations of the Virgin Queen." *Renaissance Quarterly* 43 (1990): 30–74.

——. *Tudor Royal Iconography: Literature and Art in an Age of Religious Crisis*. Princeton, N.J., 1989.

Kipling, Rudyard. *Complete Verse*. Defin. ed. New York, 1989.

Knowles, David, and R. N. Hadcock. *Medieval Religious Houses: England and Wales*. London, 1971.

Knox, John. *First Blast of the Trumpet against the Monstrous Regiment of Women*. Geneva, 1558.

Koht, Halvdan. "The Dawn of Nationalism in Europe." *American Historical Review* 52 (January 1947): 265–80.

Kristeva, Julia. "Stabat Mater." In Suleiman, *The Female Body in Western Culture*. Trans. Arthur Goldhammer of Kristeva, "Héréthique de l'amour," *Tel Quel* 74 (1977); also in Kristeva, *Histoires d'amour* (Paris, 1983).

Kroebner, R. "'The Imperial Crown of this Realm': Henry VIII, Constantine the Great, and Polydore Vergil." *Bulletin of the Institute for Historical Research* 26 (1953): 29–52.

Kurath, Hans, Sherman M. Kuhn, and John Reidy, eds. *Middle English Dictionary*. Ann Arbor, Mich., 1956– .

Lacy, John [disputed authorship]. *A Middle English Treatise on the Ten Commandments.* Ed. James Finch Royster. *Studies in Philology* 6 (1910): 9–35.

Lamb, Mary Ellen. "Cooke Sisters: Attitudes toward Learned Women in the Renaissance." In Hannay, *Silent but for the Word.*

Langlois, Ch. V. "Instrumenta facta super examinatione M. Porete, culpabilis de heresi." *Revue historique* 54 (1894): 295–99.

Lanyer, Aemilia [Bassano]. *Salve deux rex judaeorum.* London, 1611.

Lea, H. C. *History of the Inquisition.* 4 vols. New York, 1907.

Leander. *Regula, sive liber de institutione virginum et contemptu mundi, ad Florentinam sororem.* PL 72:874–94.

Leclerq, Jean. *Monks and Love in Twelfth-Century France: Psycho-Historical Essays.* Oxford, 1979.

Le Fèvre, Raoul. *The Recuyell of the Historyes of Troye.* Trans. William Caxton. Bruges, 1475.

Leff, Gordon. *Heresy in the Later Middle Ages: The Relation of Heterodoxy to Dissent, c. 1250–1450.* 2 vols. New York, 1967.

Lefranc, Abel. *A la découverte de Shakespeare.* Paris, 1950.

——. *Les Idées religieuses de Marguerite de Navarre d'après son oeuvre poétique.* Paris, 1898.

——. *Sous le masque de Shakespeare.* Paris, 1918.

Leland, John. *Assertio inclytissimii Arturii, regis Britanniae.* London, 1544.

Lesellier, J. "Deux Enfants naturels de Rabelais legitimés par le pape Paul III." *Humanisme et Renaissance* 5 (1938): 549–70.

Letters and Papers, Foreign and Domestic, of the Reign of Henry VIII, 1509–1547. Ed. James Gairdner and R. H. Brodie. 21 vols. London, 1862–1910.

Levin, Carole. "Queens and Claimants: Political Insecurity in Sixteenth Century England." In *Gender Ideology and Action: Historical Perspectives on Women's Lives,* ed. Janet Sharistanian, pp.41–66. Westport, Conn., 1986.

Lévi-Strauss, Claude. *The Elementary Structures of Kinship.* Ed. Rodney Needham, trans. James Harle Bell and John Richard von Sturmer. Boston, 1969.

Lewalski, Barbara K. "Of God and Good Women: The Poems of Aemelia Lanyer." In Hannay, *Silent but for the Word.*

Lewis, Bernard. *The Political Language of Islam.* Chicago, 1988.

Lincoln, Victoria. *Teresa, a Woman: A Biography of Teresa of Avila.* Intro. Antonio T. de Nicholás. Albany, N.Y., 1984.

Lingard, John. *The History of England from the First Invasion by the Romans to the Accession of William and Mary in 1688.* 10 vols. London, 1883.

Livy, Titus. *The Romane History.* Trans. Philemon Holland. London, 1600.

Locke, John. *Two Treatises on Civil Government.* Intro. W. S. Carpenter. 1924; rpt. London, 1953.

Lucas de Penna. *Commentaria in tres libros codicis.* Lyon, 1544, 1597.

Luther, Martin. "Against the Antinomians." Trans. Martin H. Bertram, intro. Franklin Sherman. LW 47:101–20.

——. *A la noblesse chrétienne de la nation allemande: La liberté du chrétien.* Ed. and trans. Maurice Graver. Bilingual ed. Paris, 1946.

——. "An Appeal to . . . the Ruling Class of German Nationality." In *Reformation Writings of Martin Luther,* trans. B. L. Woolf. London, 1952.

——. "The Estate of Marriage." Trans. Walther I. Brandt. LW 45:17–49.

——. "Exhortation to All Clergy Assembled at Augsburg." Trans. Lewis W. Spitz. LW 34:9–62.

——. "An Exhortation to the Knights of the Teutonic Order That They Lay Aside False Chastity and Assume the True Chastity of Wedlock." Trans. Albert T. W. Steinhaeuser, rev. Walther I. Brandt. LW 45:141–58.

——. "The Persons Related by Consanguinity and Affinity Who

Are Forbidden to Marry According to the Scriptures, Leviticus 18." Trans. Walther I. Brandt. LW 45:7–9.

———. *Tischreden.* 6 vols. Weimar, 1912–21.

Lydgate, John. *Fall of Princes* (1431–38). 4 vols. Ed. Henry Bergen. Washington, D.C., 1923.

McCusker, H. C. *John Bale, Dramatist and Antiquary.* Freeport, N.Y., 1971.

McDonnell, Ernest W. *The Beguines and Beghards: With Special Emphasis on the Belgian Scene.* New York, 1969.

MacDougall, Hugh A. *Racial Myth in English History: Trojans, Teutons, and Anglo-Saxons.* Hanover, N.H., 1982.

McKerrow, R. B., *Dictionary of Printers and Booksellers: 1557–1640.* London, 1910.

Madan, Falconer. *A Summary Catalogue of Western Manuscripts in the Bodleian Library at Oxford.* Oxford, 1895.

Mansi, J. D., ed. *Sacrorum conciliorum nova et amplissima collectio.* 31 vols. Florence, 1759–98.

Mangenot, [Joseph-]Eugene. "Inceste." In Vacant, Mangenot, and Amann, *Dictionnaire de théologie catholique,* 7:1539–56.

Marguerite de Navarre (Marguerite d'Angoulême). *L'Heptameron des nouvelles.* Ed. Le Roux de Lincy and Anatole de Montaiglon. 4 vols. Paris, 1880.

———. *Heptameron.* Trans. and intro. George Saintsbury. 5 vols. London, 1894.

———. *Marguerites de la Marguerite des princesses tresillustre royne de Navarre.* Ed. S. Sylvius. Lyon, 1547.

———. *Le Miroir de l'âme pécheresse: Discord étant en l'homme par contrariété de l'esprit et de la chair.* Ed. Joseph L. Allaire. Munich, 1972. (Variorum edition: See Salmineu, *Le Miroir de l'âme pécheresse.*)

———. *La Navire; ou, Consolation du roi François Ier a sa soeur Marguerite.* Ed. Robert Marichal. Paris, 1956.

———. *Les Prisons.* Ed. Simone Glasson. Geneva, 1978.

——. *Les Prisons*. Ed. Claire Lynch Wade. Bilingual ed. American University Studies II, Romance Languages and Literature 99. New York, 1989.

——. *The Queene of Nauarres tales*. Oxford, 1597.

Martialis, Marcus Valerius. *Epigrammaton libri*. Kingston (?), 1615.

Martin, Edward. *A History of the Iconoclast Controversy*. New York, 1930.

Matthews, C. M. "The True Cymbeline." *History Today* 7 (1957): 755–59.

Matthiessen, F. O. *Translation: An Elizabethan Art*. New York, 1965.

Mayer, Anton L. *"Mater et filia." Jahrbüch für Liturgiewissenschaft* 7 (1927): 60–82.

Melanchthon [Schwarzerd], Philip. *Unterricht der Visitatorn an die Pfarhern*. Pref. Martin Luther. Wittenberg, 1527.

Melville, Herman. *Pierre; or, The Ambiguities* (1852). Ed. Henry A. Murray. New York, 1964.

Michelet, Jules. *Histoire de France*, vol.8, *Reformé*. In *Oeuvres complètes*. Paris, 1893.

Middleton, Thomas. *The Family of Love*. Ed. Simon Shepherd. Nottingham, 1979.

Mill, John Stuart. *On Liberty, The Subjection of Women, and Representative Government*. London, 1912.

Millin, Aubin Louis. *Antiquités nationales*. 5 vols. Paris, 1790–99.

Montaigne. *Essayes*. Trans. John Florio. London, 1603.

Montalembert, Charles Forbes René de Tyron. *The Monks of the West from St. Benedict to St. Bernard*. 7 vols. Edinburgh, 1861–79.

Montrose, Louis Adrian. "Shaping Fantasies: Figurations of Gender and Power in Elizabethan Culture." *Representations* 1 (1983): 61–94.

More, Thomas. *Confutacyon with Tindale*. Vol.8, pt.1, of *The Complete Works of St. Thomas More*, ed. Louis A. Schuster, Richard C. Marius, James P. Lusardi, and Richard J. Schoeck. New Haven, Conn., 1973.

——. *Utopia* (1516). Ed. Joseph Hirst Lupton. Oxford, 1895.

Morison, Samuel Eliot. *The Oxford History of the American People.* New York, 1965.

Morning Chronicle (London). C. 1700– .

Mulcaster, Richard. *Positions . . . for the Training Up of Children.* London, 1581.

Mumby, Frank A. *The Girlhood of Queen Elizabeth: A Narrative in Contemporary Letters.* London, 1909.

Murray, Frances. "Feminine Spirituality in the More Household." *Moreana* 27–28 (1970): 92–100.

Mutschmann, Heinrich, and Karl Wentersdorf. *Shakespeare and Catholicism.* New York, 1952.

Nashe, Thomas. *The Works of Thomas Nashe.* Ed. R. B. McKerrow. 5 vols. London, 1910.

Naz, R., ed. *Dictionnaire de droit canonique.* Paris, 1935.

Neale, John Ernest. *Elizabeth I and her Parliaments, 1559–1581.* London, 1953.

——. *Queen Elizabeth: A Biography.* London, 1935; New York, 1957.

New Catholic Encyclopedia. 15 vols. New York, 1967.

Nicholas I. *Responses to the Questions of the Bulgars.* In Mansi, *Sacrorum conciliorum,* vol.15.

Norbrook, David. *Poetry and Politics in the English Renaissance.* London, 1984.

Norena, Carlos G. *Juan Luis Vives.* The Hague, 1970.

Onslow, Richard William Alan. *Empress Maud.* London, 1939.

On ureisun of Ure Louerde. In *Ye wohunge of Ure Lauerd . . . ,* ed. W. Meredith Thompson. EETS. London, 1958.

Oxford Latin Dictionary. Ed. P. G. W. Glare. Oxford, 1982.

Parr, Catherine. *The Lamentacion of a Synner.* London, 1547.

——. *Prayers, or Meditations.* London, 1545.

——. *Prayers stirryng the mynd vnto heuvenlye meditacions.* London, 1545.

Parrington, Vernon L. *The Romantic Revolution in America: 1800–1860.* New York, 1954.

Partridge, Marianne. "Good Queen Bess." *New York Times Book Review,* 17 March 1991, p.26.

Patristic Greek Lexicon. Ed. G. W. H. Lampe. Oxford, 1964.

Perrens, F. T. *Les libertins en France au XVIIe siècle.* 1896; New York, 1973.

Pits, John. *Relationum historicum de rebus Anglia.* Paris, 1619.

Pius XII. "Sponsa Christi." *Acta Apostolicae Sedis* 43 (1951): 5–37.

Pole, Reginald (Cardinal). *Ad Henricum VIII . . . pro ecclesiasticae unitatis defensione* (1536). In Rocaberti, *Bibliotheca pontifica.*

Poliakov, Leon. *The Aryan Myth.* Brighton, 1974.

Pomerius, Henry. "De origine monasterii Viridvallis." *Analecta Bollandiana* 4 (1885–86): 263–322.

Ponticus Virunius. *Britannicae historiae libri vi.* Caxton Society. London, 1844.

Porete, Marguerite. *Miroir des simples ames.* Ed. Romana Guarnieri. In Guarnieri, *Il movimento del libero spirito,* pp.150–285. Rome, 1965.

———. Middle English translation of the *Miroir.* MS 71, St. John's College, Cambridge.

———. *A Mirror for Simple Souls by a French Mystic of the Thirteenth Century.* Ed. and trans. Charles Crawford. Dublin, 1981.

———. *The Mirror of Simple Souls, by an Unknown French Mystic of the Thirteenth Century.* Ed. Clare Kirchenberger, trans. M. N. London, 1927.

Prescott, Anne Lake. "The Pearl of the Valois and Elizabeth I." In Hannay, *Silent but for the Word.*

Pringle, Roger, ed. *A Portrait of Elizabeth I in the Words of the Queen and Her Contemporaries.* Totowa, N.J., 1980.

Rabanus Maurus. *Concilium moguntium.* In Mansi, *Sacrorum conciliorum,* 14:900–912.

Rabelais, François. *Oeuvres complètes.* Ed. Pierre Jourda. 2 vols. Paris, 1962.

Racine, Jean. *Britannicus.* Ed. Philip Butler. Cambridge, 1967.

Rank, Otto. *Das Inzest-Motiv in Dichtung und Sage.* 1912; Darmstadt, 1974.

Rastell, John. *The Pastyme of People.* London, 1811.

Robert of Gloucester. *The Life and Martyrdom of Thos. Beket.* Ed. William Henry Black. Percy Society vol.19. London, 1845.

Rocaberti, Juan T. *Bibliotheca pontifica.* Rome, 1689.

Rogers, John. *The Displaying of an Horrible Secte of [Grosse and Wicked] Heretiques, Naming Themselves the Familie of Love.* London, 1578.

Rolle, Richard. *Form of Living.* C. 1425. In *Yorkshire Writers,* ed. Carl Horstmann, vol.1. London, 1895.

Rose, Mary Beth, ed. *Women in the Middle Ages and the Renaissance: Literary and Historical Perspectives.* Syracuse, N.Y., 1986.

Rosenblatt, Jason P. "Aspects of the Incest Problems in *Hamlet.*" *Shakespeare Quarterly* 29 (1978): 349–64.

Sackville, Thomas Dorset, and Thomas Norton. *The Tragedie of Gorboduc, whereof Three Actes Were Written by Thomas Nortone and the Two Laste by Thomas Sackwyle.* London, 1565.

Sade, Donatien Alphonse François, Comte de. *La Philosophie dans le boudoir.* 1795; Paris, 1972.

Saffady, William. "Fears of Sexual License during the English Reformation." *History of Childhood Quarterly* 1 (1973): 89–97.

Salminen, Renja. Commentary. In Marguerite de Navarre, *Le Miroir de l'âme pécheresse: Edition critique et commentaire suivis de la traduction faite par la princesse Elizabeth future reigne d'Angleterre, "The Glasse of the Sinful Soule,"* ed. Renja Salminen. *Dissertations Humanarum Litterarum* (Annales Academiae Fennicae), no.22. Helsinki, 1979.

Saxl, Fritz, and Rudolph Wittkower. *British Art and the Mediterranean.* Oxford, 1948.

Bibliography of Works Cited

Saxo Grammaticus. *Historiae Danicae*. In *The Sources of "Hamlet," with an Essay on the Legend*, ed. Israel Gollancz. London, 1926.

Schleiner, Winfried. "*Divina Virago*: Queen Elizabeth as an Amazon." *Studies in Philology* 75 (1978): 163–80.

Schneider, Gerhard. *Der Libertin: Zur Geistes- und Sozialgeschichte des Bürgerturns im 16. und 17. Jahrhundert*. Stuttgart, 1970.

Sckommodau, H. "Die religiösen Dichtungen Margarete von Navarra." *Arbeitsgemeinschaft für Forschung des Landes Nordrhein Westfalen* 36 (1955).

Screech, M. A. *The Rabelaisian Marriage: Aspects of Rabelais's Religion, Ethics, and Comic Philosophy*. London, 1958.

Seymour, Anne, Jane Seymour, and Margaret Seymour. *Mortum Margaritas Valesiae: Navorrorum Reginae, Hecatadistichon. . . .* Paris, 1550. French trans. *Le Tombeau de Marguerite de Valois* (1551).

Seymour, William. *Ordeal by Ambition: An English Family in the Shadow of the Tudors*. London, 1972.

Shakespeare, William. *Complete Works of Shakespeare*. Ed. George Lyman. Kittredge. Boston, 1936.

——. *All's Well That Ends Well*. Ed. Sylvan Barnett. New York, 1965.

——. *Hamlet*. Ed. William Farnham. Baltimore, Md., 1966.

——. *Hamlet*. Ed. Harold Jenkins. London, 1982.

——. *King Henry the Eighth*. Ed. R. A. Foakes. London, 1968.

——. *Love's Labor's Lost*. Ed. Richard David. London, 1966.

——. *Measure for Measure*. Ed. J. W. Lever, London, 1965.

——. *Pericles of Tyre*. Ed. F. D. Hoeniger. London, 1963.

——. *Richard the Third*. In *The Complete Works of Shakespeare*, 3d ed., ed. David Bevington. Glenview, Ill., 1980.

Shell, Marc. *Children of the Earth: Literature, Politics, and Nationhood*. Oxford University Press, forthcoming 1993.

——. *The End of Kinship: "Measure for Measure," Incest, and the Ideal of Universal Siblinghood*. Stanford, Calif., 1988.

——. *Money, Language, and Thought: Literary and Philosophical Economies from the Medieval to the Modern Era*. Berkeley, Calif., 1982.

———. "Those Extraordinary Twins." *Arizona Quarterly* 47, no.2 (1991): 29–75.

Smith, Charles Edward. *Papal Enforcement of Some Medieval Marriage Laws.* 1940; Port Washington, N.Y., 1972.

Smith, Nigel, ed. *A Collection of Ranter Writings from the 17th Century.* Foreword John Carey. London, 1983.

Snyder, Louis L. *The Idea of Racialism.* New York, 1962.

Speed, John. *The History of Great Britain.* London, 1614.

Stanley, Diane, and Peter Vennema. *The Story of Elizabeth I of England.* New York, 1990.

Staves, Susan. *Players' Scepters: Fiction of Authority in the Restoration.* Lincoln, Neb., 1979.

Steele, R. "English Books Printed Abroad, 1525–48." *Transactions of the Bibliographical Society* 11 (1909): 189–236.

Stenton, Doris May. *The English Women in History.* London, 1957.

Stephan of Tournai. *Summa decreti.* Ed. J. F. von Schulte. Giessen, 1891.

Stone, Lawrence. *Crisis of the Aristocracy, 1558–1641.* Oxford, 1965.

Strong, Roy C. *The Cult of Elizabeth.* London, 1977.

———. *Portraits of Queen Elizabeth.* Oxford, 1963.

Swaim, M. H. "A New Year's Gift from the Princess Elizabeth." *The Connoisseur,* August 1973, pp.258–66.

Tacitus, Publius [Gaius Cornelius]. *The Annals of Imperial Rome.* Trans. Michael Grant. Harmondsworth, Eng., 1977.

Tatlock, J. S. P. *The Legendary History of Britain: Geoffrey of Monmouth's Historia Regum Britanniae and Its Early Vernacular Versions.* Berkeley, Calif., 1950.

Taylor, Gary. General Introduction. In *The Complete Oxford Shakespeare.* Ed. W. Stanley Wells, 3 vols. New York, 1987.

Taylor, Mark. *Shakespeare's Darker Purpose: A Question of Incest.* New York, 1982.

Telle, Emile. *L'Oeuvre de Marguerite d'Angoulême, reine de Navarre, et La Querelle des femmes.* Toulouse, 1937.

———. "L'Île des alliances, ou l'anti-Thélème." *Bibliothèque d'Humanisme et Renaissance* 14 (1952): 159–75.

Tennenhouse, Leonard. "Representing Power: *Measure for Measure* in Its Time." *Genre* 15 (1982): 139–56.

Teresa of Jesus. *The Complete Works of Saint Teresa of Jesus.* Trans. E. Allison Peers. 3 vols. London, 1946.

Tertullian. *Apologeticus.* CC 185–171.

Travitsky, Betty. *The Paradise of Women: Writings by Englishwomen of the Renaissance.* New York, 1989.

Turner, Sharon. *History of the Anglo-Saxons.* Vol.3. London, 1828.

Twine, L. *The Patterne of Painefull Adventures* (c. 1594). In *Shakespeare's Library*, 2d ed., ed. John Payne Collier, vol.4. London, 1875.

Tyrwhitt, Elizabeth. *Morning and Euening Prayers, with Diuvers Psalmes, Himnes, and Meditations.* London, 1574.

Vacant, A., E. Mangenot, and E. Amann, eds. *Dictionnaire de théologie catholique.* 23 vols. Paris, 1923–72.

Vautrollier, Thomas. *Luther's Commentarie ypon the Epistle to the Galatians.* 1575, 1577.

Vergil, Polydore. *Angelica historia* [1534]. Ed. and trans. Denys Hay. Camden Society, 3d ser., 74. London, 1950.

Verstegen, Richard. *A Restitution of Decayed Intelligence in Antiquities concerning the Most Noble and Renowned English Nation.* 1605; London, 1673.

Vest, Walter E. "William Shakespeare, Syphilographer." *West Virginia Medical Journal* 34, no.1 (1938): 130–37.

Vico, Giovanni Battista. *Principles of New Science of Giovanni Battista Vico concerning the Nature of the Nations.* Rev. trans. of 3d ed. (1744). Trans. and ed. Thomas Goddard Bergin and Max Harold Fish. Ithaca, N.Y., 1968.

Viller, Marcel, et al. *Dictionnaire de spiritualité.* Paris, 1937.

Bibliography of Works Cited

Vives, Juan Luis. *De institutione foeminae Christiane.* Trans. as *The Instruction of a Christian Woman.* London, 1529.

Walker, Williston. *John Calvin: The Organizer of Reformed Protestantism.* New York, 1969.

Walpole, Horace. *A Catalogue of the Royal and Noble Authors of England* (1758). 5 vols. Ed. Thomas Park. London, 1806.

Warner, Marina. *Alone of All Her Sex: The Myth and Cult of the Virgin Mary.* London, 1976.

Wells, Robin Headlam. *Spenser's "Faerie Queene" and the Cult of Elizabeth.* London, 1988.

Wells, Stanley. *Modernizing Shakespeare's Spelling.* In Gary Taylor, *Three Studies in the Text of "Henry V."* Oxford, 1979.

Wels, L. E. *Theologische Streifzüge durch die älfranzosiche Literatur.* Vechta, 1937.

Westermarck, Edward. *The History of Human Marriage.* 5th ed. 3 vols. New York, 1922.

Whibley, Charles. "Translators." In *The Cambridge History of English Literature,* ed. A. W. Ward and A. R. Walker, 4:1–25. New York, 1909.

Wiesner, Merry E. "Beyond Women and the Family: Toward Gender Analysis of the Reformation." *Sixteenth Century Journal* 18, no.3 (1987): 311–21.

Wilkinson, W. *A Supplication of the Family of Love . . . Examined, and Found Derogatorie in an Hie Degree.* London, 1606.

Williams, Neville. *Elizabeth, Queen of England.* London, 1967.

Willibald of Mainz. *Vita S. Bonifacii.* PL 89:603–32.

Wright, C. E. "The Dispersal of the Monastic Libraries and the Beginnings of Anglo-Saxon Studies." *Transaction of the Cambridge Bibliographical Society* 1 (1951): 208–37.

Writings of Ed[ward] VI, William Hugh, Queen Catherine Parr, Anne Askew, Lady Jane Grey, Hamilton and Balnaves. Philadelphia, 1862.

Bibliography of Works Cited

Wycliffe, John. *Two Short Treatises against the Order of the Begging Friars.* Oxford, 1608.

Yablonsky, Lewis. *The Hippie Trip.* Baltimore, Md., 1973.

Yates, F. A. *Astraea: The Imperial Theme in the Sixteenth Century.* London, 1975.

Index

Aaron (Bible), 320

Abelard, Peter, 306

Adam (Bible), 14, 21

Adoption: and adrogation, 21, 59, 315; by God, 26, 35, 40, 56, 59, 315

Aelred of Rievaulx, 311

Aeneas, 60, 77

Agrippina, 59, 60, 315, 317

Ailly, Pierre (Bishop), 308

Alfred (King), 62, 300

Ambrose (Saint), 323

Ames, Percy, 30, 297, 307

Ancrene Riwle, 307

Andreas, Bernardus (historian), 77, 322

Andrew (brother of Bernard of Clairvaux), 38

Angoulême, Duke of (Francis's son), 19

Anne (Saint), 317–18

Anne of Cleaves, 8, 17

Anthony (Saint), 37

Antigone, 16

Apollonius of Tyre, 301

Aquinas, Thomas (Saint), 52, 65, 318

Archpriest controversy, 54, 314

Aristotle, 65, 313, 318

Ascham, Roger, 293, 295

Ashley, Mistress, 299

Ashley, Thomas, 299

Askew, Anne, 4, 47, 48, 49, 62, 79, 81, 310, 317

Athanasius (Saint), 305, 309

Augereau, Antoine, 291

Augustine (Saint), 79, 317, 322

Augustus Caesar, 54, 59

Aurelius, Marcus, 317

Baker, Richard, 72, 321

Bakhtin, Mikhail, 311, 312

Balbus, Bernardus (Bishop), 298

Bale, John: conversion of, 79, 292; early life of, 292; edits *Glass*, 4; exile of, 67; marries Sister Dorothy, 296, 306; prebendary of Canterbury, 107; as Protestant polemicist, 3; as scholar, 3–4. *Works:* "Conclusion," (Elizabeth), 4, 26, 34, 47, 77, 79, 81, 107, 298, 302, 314, 317, 318; *Elucidation* (Askew), 310, 317; "Epistle Dedicatory" (Elizabeth), 4, 22, 34, 77, 79, 81, 107, 311, 314, 316, 317; *Illustrium*, 292; *Image of Both Churches*, 41, 79, 306; *Kynge Johann*, 5, 64, 292; *Three Laws of Nature*, 41; *Vocacyon*, 317

Bandinelli, Orlando (Alexander III), 298

Basil (Saint), 37

Basileus, 323

Bastardy (bastardization): and carnal contagion; and fornication/incest, 8–12, 14; James V as bastardizing,

355

Index

Index

Index